MAXAND HARVEY
(in a BOOK)

PUFFIN

AUTUMN

MEET MAX AND HARVEY

HARVEY: I'm two minutes older than Max – I'm the eldest so I take that responsibility seriously!

MAX: We were born in Berkshire on 31 December 2002.

HARVEY: We had terrible childhoods. We lived in a cage. Only joking! Dad was a singer in West End shows and musicals. He had to tour a lot, and for our first birthday and Christmas he was in Germany with a show. I think that was quite hard for him and Mum so he quit and got a 'real' job. We're close to both our parents. Mum is there for us emotionally, and Dad is there practically – he's better at homework and stuff! And he's from a performing background so he's really supportive in that respect.

MAX: Mum and Dad met on cruise ships, where they were entertainers. We were a surprise! When our mum found out she was pregnant she wasn't thrilled – and when she was told we were twins she cried! But she loves us now, and she's the best mum.

HARVEY: People always ask us whether we like being twins. There are pros and cons. There's always someone your age to hang out with. And we never

feel like we don't have our own personalities. Our mum has always worked really hard to make sure we have our own space – we're in different classes at school, and both our parents spend time with us separately.

MAX: We're pretty equal at most things, so when we're just at home and not with our mates it's good to play football and stuff.

HARVEY: I'm so bad at cricket though!

MAX: He had the worst injury I've ever seen – he got hit by a ball in the throat! But generally we're pretty evenly matched.

HARVEY: We've lived in our house since we were three. We moved there when Mum was pregnant with our little brother, Leo.

MAX: We used to not get on with him that well! We do now though. He used to be such a wind-up merchant and got us into trouble all the time, but now he's much better.

HARVEY: He's at boarding school, and we miss him quite a lot. I think if he wasn't away at school we might fight all the time! But we really like it when we see him now.

MAX: And then we have another sibling: our little sister, Tilly. We were eight when she was born.

HARVEY: She's all right most of the time.

MAX: For such a tiny person, she's very loud! I get on with her best. She's good when I look after her but not when Harvey does – when I put her to bed she goes to sleep right away. I love all my siblings – though three children would have been enough! But Mum wanted a girl. I really wanted Leo to be a girl, so when he was born I had a strop!

HARVEY: I wanted him to be a boy so I didn't mind! Leo is really good at singing. He's in a choir at his school, and we often go and see him sing. And from as soon as we could play and sing Max and I have been musical. When Dad was in shows we always used to go along to rehearsals.

MAX: We actually got our first professional jobs when we were babies – we were in a TV show at nine months old! And we did stuff like that until we were about two.

HARVEY: Mum got us some cool work when we were babies – if you're twins you get cast, especially if you're identical. It was never the plan for us to carry on after

that, but we just really enjoyed it and our school work didn't suffer, and we've met so many cool people that we didn't really want to stop! I mean, it sort of did interfere with school sometimes when we had to do a lot of performances, but my teachers just thought it was cool – they all came to see me.

MAX: We started at drama school when we were four, so we've been doing it for ten years. We love it so much: performing is our favourite hobby, so it has never felt like work – even when technically it *has* been. We've done some really random stuff! When I was about nine I did an advert for Google in Brazil. We filmed it in the UK unfortunately! It was so much fun – I got to ride down a hill in a go-kart powered by fire extinguishers! I've never found the advert, but I'd love to see it. I think I might have been cut out.

HARVEY: I was the voice of VTech toys for a while: I was a green dog called Scout! I was eight. We used to go into Toys 'R' Us and Tesco and press all the toys and my voice would come out! It was so normal doing work like that though – we've always really enjoyed it and never wanted to stop. Things just kept coming up.

MAX: We did a short film about twins for Channel 4, and we did amateur shows with our drama club and at school.

7

HARVEY: I first got to be in a professional show when I was about eight – I was in *Priscilla Queen of the Desert* in the West End. I'm so glad I did it – it was fun, even though Mum had just had Tilly and she had to drive me everywhere with the baby in the car seat. It was a really exciting and different experience. My solo was right at the end of the show, so I didn't need to be at the theatre until really late every night. It was brilliant driving down to London after school, and performing in a real theatre.

MAX: I was Gavroche in an adaptation of *Les Misérables* at the same time. I got to go on tour to the Edinburgh Fringe Festival, which was crazy and so much fun. We both auditioned for *Billy Elliott* as well, but we didn't get that. Which is just as well because we would have had to rehearse in the summer holidays! That is a really hard part to play.

HARVEY: After *Priscilla* finished, I was in *Les Mis* playing the same part as Max. That was when we were about nine. It was cool to share that role. And then, when we were twelve, we went on tour with *The Sound of Music* – we alternated the role of Friedrich. That was awesome, and it was crazy to be in a different place every night.

MAX: We don't audition any more these days – we have too much going on outside school – but we used to really enjoy it. We'd take a trip up to London and get to meet new people and sing and stuff. We've made so many friends in drama school through the years – it's been great for us.

HARVEY: Yeah, it's made us more mature . . . I like to think so, anyway!

MAX: And in March 2016 we started on Musical.ly. And that changed everything, even though we could never, ever have imagined that it would at the time.

HARVEY: Our school friends who are twins made us join! We enjoyed it right from the beginning. It was just so easy to use that we didn't think anything of making a few videos every day. Our parents are interested in everything we do so they knew what we were up to and made sure we were safe – and it's just sort of grown from there.

MAX: We were on holiday with our friend in LA and he gave us a shout out on Musical.ly – we both had individual accounts. But we were making so many videos together on holiday and enjoying it so much that we started a joint account. We did a video of us singing together, and it got featured on the app globally, and then people were really nice about it and we just grew really quickly.

HARVEY: I'd always wanted to put music to videos

2016

JANUARY   Joined Musical.ly with individual accounts

FEBRUARY   Finished *The Sound of Music* UK Tour where we had been alternating the role of Friedrich

MARCH   Set up Musical.ly 'MaxandHarveyOfficial' account

First feature on Musical.ly within two weeks of setting up account

APRIL   100,000 fans on Musical.ly

MAY   Set up YouTube and Instagram official accounts

300,000 fans on Musical.ly

JUNE   Set up Twitter and Facebook official accounts

500,000 fans on Musical.ly

JULY   Invited to perform at Camp Bestival on 'The Den' stage

1 MILLION fans on Musical.ly

AUGUST   Holiday in the south of France where we were recognized while busking in Cannes and St Tropez

100,000 followers on Instagram

SEPTEMBER Salon International gig at London Excel Centre in front of 1,000+ people

1.5 million fans on Musical.ly

– it was so easy on Musical.ly. We were really surprised when we got so well known – we didn't know what to do, but we've learned along the way, which has been fun. Look at all the crazy stuff that happened in 2016!

OCTOBER First TV appearance for Swipe TV on RTL in Ireland

100,000 followers on Facebook

2 MILLION fans on Musical.ly

NOVEMBER Headline fireworks night gig in front of 10,000 people in our home town

Release first music video – Shawn Mendes mash-up cover of 'Stitches' / 'Treat You Better'

100,000 subscribers on YouTube

200,000 followers on Instagram

DECEMBER First ever Max and Harvey gig, and meet and greet at The Seahorse Cafe in West Sussex

Release Christmas song video of 'I Wish It Could Be Christmas'

Release own original song 'One More Day in Love' – written by us!

150,000 subscribers on YouTube

250,000 followers on Instagram

2.75 million fans on Musical.ly

MAX: It's especially mad when you think we hadn't really been on social media before. We had YouTube, but we were only allowed to use our dad's account and we only posted covers. But we put up loads of videos of us busking. And now it's lots more professional!

HARVEY: We only started in March 2016, but by the end of the year it was a massive thing for us – we had over three million followers. Social media is crazy like that. And now it's really exciting. We don't want to stop – we want to see where it takes us. We have amazing fans.

MAX: It's weird having people recognize us sometimes. We love seeing them. And loads of them are really talented and post covers of our songs, which is my favourite thing ever.

HARVEY: Everyone's so dedicated and nice – it's lovely that there are so many supportive people out there. They do all these things for us that take so much time, which is crazy – a year ago not a single one would have known who we are, and now we have this new community from an app we'd never heard of. We've met so many incredible people out of it.

MAX: So because things have changed so much this year, we wanted to keep a diary. And we really wanted to share it with people!

HARVEY: 2016 was a crazy year for us.

MAX: Yeah, we had no idea this was going to happen.

HARVEY: The weirdest thing is how normal it all is, but we're learning loads of new, fun stuff too. What we really want to do is write music and we get to do that now – we're meeting professional writers. And we're still posting a lot, and sometimes we're doing collabs or even interviews for radio and magazines and stuff.

MAX: But at the same time we're still at school, and we've got the same mates we've had for years, so none of them care at all. This year has been really interesting. We've always balanced performing with school so it doesn't feel new to us, but it's different now.

HARVEY: Mainly because there are so many people who know who we are, and literally no one had heard of us before. It's incredible how quickly social media can change your life. I feel lucky to be a twin so I don't have to do it on my own.

MAX: Mostly we love it, but sometimes it can be a little overwhelming.

HARVEY: And we're even filming it for the BBC!

MAX: So we're writing it all down – we want to remember everything and share it with all of you as it happens . . .

MAX AND HARVEY'S BUCKET LISTS

MAX:

1. Skydive
2. Perform with Major Lazer
3. Meet Ariana Grande
4. Meet every single one of our fans
5. Play the O2 arena
6. Play Glastonbury
7. Travel the world performing
8. Get a pet snake!
9. Live in LA
10. Buy a motorbike and learn to ride it

HARVEY:

1. Skydive
2. Perform in the London O2 arena
3. Become a presenter
4. Meet Logan Paul
5. Write a song with Skrillex
6. Do a world tour
7. Have a number 1 song
8. Headline Glastonbury
9. Collab with Ed Sheeran
10. Raise £1,000,000 for a charity

31 DECEMBER 2016: MAX AND HARVEY'S 14TH BIRTHDAY!

MAX: We're starting this diary on our birthday – just before the new year. Seems like a good place to begin! People think it's weird to have your birthday on 31 December, but I really like it. It's quite cool because every year we basically get a free firework display, and it feels like everyone's celebrating our birthday! And this year we got some awesome presents.

HARVEY: I had some cool T-shirts for my birthday, and Max and I got a Segway to share.

MAX: And I had a new camera thing for my phone.

HARVEY: Things have changed a lot since our last birthday. Back then we were doing the *Sound of Music* tour, and now we're still doing music and performing, but in a different way. Our birthday was better this year because we got to spend the whole day together. Last year Max was doing a show, so we couldn't.

MAX: Yes, last year I was doing a show in Manchester, but today was different – we went to see *Aladdin* in London.

HARVEY: It was so amazing!

MAX: This year we got to see all our family on our birthday too, because we'd celebrated Christmas a bit later than normal. Our little brother, Leo, was singing in a choir in Windsor (where the Queen lives!) on Christmas Day, so we had to have our real Christmas the day after – we were watching Leo all day on the 25th. We only had one Christmas present on the actual day – it was weird!

HARVEY: It was good to see the rest of our family – it's been such a crazy year, and we hadn't seen our cousins for ages. We made some videos with them and played some songs for our auntie, because it was also her 50th birthday.

MAX: It was a really fun day, hanging out with our family at her party. We're really close to them. And now we're excited about the year ahead!

NEW YEAR'S RESOLUTIONS

MAX: I never have New Year's resolutions – it's quite stressful and you feel like people are just trying to judge you if you fail! I prefer to change without realizing it.

HARVEY: My New Year's resolution is to keep working as hard as possible. We are so lucky to be able to do something we love so much, so I want to make the most of it!

MAX AND HARVEY'S BEST PRESENTS

MAX:

1. A guitar
2. A Segway
3. CHOCOLATE!
4. A trampoline (we got it when we were really young)

HARVEY:

1. A puppet (I loved that when I was 10)
2. An Osmo gimbal for my phone
3. A Segway
4. Clothes

MAX'S FAVOURITE...

COLOUR:	turquoise
ANIMAL:	monkey
LUCKY NUMBER:	2
SONG:	too many to choose – probably 'Bad' by David Guetta
POPSTAR/BAND:	Coldplay
FRUIT:	lemon
FOOD:	bacon bits
VEGETABLE:	cucumber
ICE CREAM:	lemon sorbet
CAKE:	red velvet

BOOK: *The Hunger Games*

FILM: *Captain America: Civil War*

ACTOR: Ryan Reynolds

ACTRESS: Megan Fox

DISNEY CHARACTER: Dopey from *Snow White and the Seven Dwarfs*

HOLIDAY: Florida

BREAKFAST: full English

DRINK: ginger beer with lemonade and loads of ice – sounds weird but, trust me, it's amazing

LAST MEAL: nachos to start, steak and ribs and chips, cookie dough with ice cream (with a side of bacon!)

HARVEY'S FAVOURITE...

COLOUR: maroon

ANIMAL: panda

LUCKY NUMBER: 7

SONG: 'Car Radio' by 21 Pilots

POPSTAR/BAND: 21 Pilots

FRUIT: pomegranate seeds

FOOD: pizza

VEGETABLE: sweetcorn

ICE CREAM: cookie dough

CAKE: red velvet

BOOK: *Divergent*

FILM: *Ant-Man*

ACTOR: Dave Franco

ACTRESS: Anna Kendrick

DISNEY CHARACTER: Genie from *Aladdin*

HOLIDAY: France

BREAKFAST: waffle and Nutella – I have it every single day!

DRINK: bubble tea

LAST MEAL: Nando's chicken wings, pizza with loads of toppings, warm chocolate brownie with ice cream

WINTER

JANUARY

MAX: It's January – we've decided to hit the ground running! We've started writing songs with a professional songwriter called Mika. It's always been a dream of ours. Harvey and I enjoy writing songs but sometimes we find it difficult to get started. We're really comfortable working with Mika – we both suggested ideas for the song we were creating. We're better at adding ideas than starting at the beginning. It's so much fun.

HARVEY: He came to us with the start of an idea, and for a couple of hours we built on it, and after that we began recording. It was great!

MAX: And we met Cassie, our manager, properly for the first time. We'd started working together a while ago, when she spotted our videos online. She began representing us when requests started to come in. But she lives in LA and it was hard to see her in person. Now we've met her at last!

HARVEY: I was really excited because we've been Skyping her so much, and it was nice to meet properly. It's such a new thing to have a manager though! It used to be our dad. But this is just such a new world.

MAX: And it was just so much work for him, on top of his proper job. Now we work with Cassie it's a lot easier – we know what we want to do and when. It's strange though; there have been sudden changes. We have a normal day at school and then a magazine interview after. At the beginning it didn't seem strange to have an audience – they were just kids on social media. And now adults are starting to interview us!

HARVEY: The strangest thing about going from an ordinary school day to doing interviews and stuff is that it feels kind of normal now. It would be weirder to chill out and do nothing! I enjoy it. I love singing and music and meeting new people so it's all fun.

MAX: School is busy too. We're in the school production of *The Sound of Music*. Harvey and I already did the UK tour of it last year, but it's different doing it with our friends! The cast at school is just as talented as the professionals. I play Friedrich and Harvey pays Rolf, who is Liesel's boyfriend. He looks a bit short in his costume, but to be fair Liesel is short too! It's fun to do it again.

HARVEY: Shows at our school are usually really good. Everything's very relaxed and it's coming together well.

MAX AND HARVEY'S FAVOURITE MUSICALS

MAX:

1. *Wicked*
2. *The Book of Mormon*
   (even though I haven't seen it – I like the soundtrack! But it's a bit rude . . .)
3. *Matilda*
4. *Les Misérables*
5. *Kinky Boots*

HARVEY:

1. *Hamilton*
2. *Aladdin*
3. *School of Rock*
4. *Blue Man Group* (it counts!)
5. *Matilda*

FAVOURITE THINGS ABOUT MUSICALS

MAX:

- The music
- The excitement of being in a theatre
- The story
- The surprises
- The different characters
- The props and scenery

HARVEY:

- They are so energetic
- The music
- The atmosphere
- The set and production – they're really cool

THE BBC

MAX: We met with the BBC after school today. A producer came to our house to ask about working together on a new show – I just can't believe we're going to be on TV! It'll be a dream come true. I like their idea for the show. It's just going to be about our lives as we start properly making music this year, showing other people our age how quickly social media can change things for you – the ups and the downs. We have complete control – I was worried it was going to be some cheesy reality show, and that definitely wouldn't make sense for us. But it would be filmed by us, when we're not performing, and show what it's like for us when these cool opportunities come up. And it'll be on TV in the autumn!

HARVEY: I'm really excited to see what happens with the BBC. I'd want to see behind the scenes in a popstar's life. I think it'll be fun to make a programme that shows people what it's really like for us – we're still really normal and at school, but we're also doing all this crazy new stuff. I hope people like it!

MAX: Yeah, it might not happen, but if it does it'll be amazing!

MAX AND HARVEY'S FAVOURITE TV SHOWS

MAX:

1. *Little Britain*
2. I used to love *SpongeBob SquarePants*
3. *I'm a Celebrity . . . Get Me Out of Here!*
4. *The Simpsons*
5. *Teletubbies* (when I was young!)

HARVEY:

1. *I'm a Celebrity . . . Get Me Out Of Here!*
2. *Little Britain*
3. *Ant and Dec's Saturday Night Takeaway*
4. James Corden's *Late Late Show*
5. *Mock the Week*
6. *Russell Howard's Good News*
7. *Hell's Kitchen*
8. *NCIS Los Angeles*
9. *Hawaii Five-0*
10. *Death in Paradise*

ALL ABOUT THE MUSIC

MAX: We met with some cool writers and producers the other day – we always work with really friendly people. These guys are called Jake Gosling and Chris Leonard, and they've worked with some massive names, like Ed Sheeran and Shawn Mendes.

HARVEY: They were really cool. I would never have guessed they worked with Ed Sheeran as writers and producers – they were so nice and kind and not at all intimidating. It's amazing – every time we do something like that we really enjoy it and learn so much. I love the atmosphere of studios, and seeing how everything works technically – I'd like to know how to do that properly. I don't have a clue what's happening!

MAX: We like to get professional help with writing songs as much as possible, just so we can improve and learn all the time. We met with some producers called Metrophonic who found a song for us to record. We only got it two days before we started recording! It takes a while to understand a song properly, and Harvey and I like to practise it loads. We're given the music and we really enjoy figuring it out together. I love going into the recording studio. It's so much fun and it helps improve our singing. Although we're recording and singing songs, the main thing we want to do is learn how to write.

MAX AND HARVEY'S FAVOURITE SONGS TO COVER

MAX:

1. 'Counting Stars'
2. 'Migraine'
3. 'Closer'
4. 'Sweet Lovin''
5. 'Stitches'

HARVEY:

1. 'Despacito'
2. 'Shape of You'
3. 'Fight Song'
4. 'Goodbye Forever'
5. 'Let Me Love You'
6. 'Pencil Full of Lead'
7. 'Counting Stars'
8. 'Sweet Lovin''
9. 'Migraine'

YOUTUBE

MAX: We've been doing loads more YouTube videos recently. I really like making them – you have more time than you do in a Musical.ly video, and we can do challenges. It makes us try new things. Making Musical.ly videos is really quick. But with YouTube it's a bit more involved. So we try a bit harder. We're doing a new challenge soon – Food Portrait Challange – that should be interesting!

HARVEY: Making YouTube videos is fun – really relaxing and kind of stupid. I enjoyed doing the one with guys trying on girls' products! It was hilarious. But I love Musical.ly – especially seeing videos that fans have made for us, when they lip-sync or cover one of our songs. It's so cool that people would do that for us. I know those things can take a long time because I do it too! It's so sweet and so much fun to watch – we really appreciate it.

MAX AND HARVEY'S TOP TIPS FOR MUSICAL.LY

MAX:

1. Be yourself
2. Make sure every video is as awesome as the last
3. Put in the effort
4. If you have no ideas for videos, look in the hashtags
5. Be creative!

HARVEY:

1. Think outside the box
2. Don't do the same thing as everyone else
3. Use the hashtags
4. Look at popular songs
5. Post regularly

MAX AND HARVEY'S TOP TIPS FOR YOUTUBE

MAX:

1. Think creatively
2. Do what you do best
3. Make sure you enjoy making the videos you make
4. Be crazy!

HARVEY:

1. Make interesting videos
2. Make sure they're not too long
3. Have an interesting thumbnail
4. Put time and effort into videos
5. Try to invest in a camera
6. Use good editing software

SHORTY AWARD

MAX: Today was INSANE! We just got nominated for a Shorty Award – we never expected that. Social media is just mad with the opportunities it gives us. There are so many millions of amazing singers in the world, and to get nominated for a music award just because of our videos is so brilliant. Musical.ly is fun for us, but it's also given us visibility so we can perform even more.

HARVEY: I am so surprised to be nominated for a Shorty. It's just really weird that suddenly people know who we are. Even being nominated just feels incredible. If we won I would just scream for days. Although that's probably a bad idea and I'd get told to stop pretty quickly!

MAX: The awards ceremony is in April in New York! I really hope we get to go.

PUPPIES

MAX: We have the best dog in the world, Pippa (we've also got a cat called Minnie). She's a golden retriever and she's in loads of our videos so you should look her up! And today she had puppies! It took ages – she started really early in the morning, but luckily it's half term so we have the rest of the day to recover.

HARVEY: Dogs have puppies after roughly nine weeks, so it's been a big build-up waiting for Pippa's, and finally they're here! There are seven – two boys and five girls, and we named them with a Disney theme for the time being. So their names are:

Genie   Belle   Moana

Tiana   Pumba   Sophia   Cinderella

MAX: They're so cute.

HARVEY: We're really hoping we get to keep one!

INTERVIEWS

HARVEY: We had an interview with an online magazine today. Sometimes interviews can be quite unnerving – you never know what questions you'll be asked, so you can't prepare anything other than the basic stuff. It's mostly fine, but if you say something in the wrong way you don't want to look stupid. Still, there are two of us! And it's fun – I like to talk to people.

MAX: And we just did our first radio interview too. I didn't get nervous or anything. It was for the BBC local radio and it was cool to visit the studio.

HARVEY: We get asked a lot of the same questions. The most-asked question is probably: *How long have you been singing together?*

MAX: So it helps that we've already got our answers! The key is just to relax, I think.

HARVEY: We've just announced that we'll be doing some live performances! We're calling them Up Close shows, and we're performing them with Hilton hotels. It's gonna be quite an interesting show because we're taking aspects of everything we do and including them. We're putting loads of thought into choosing stuff and making it different. So, for example, one thing we're hoping to do is called 'four chords': basically you play four chords on a guitar and sing any song to those four chords. So you get people to request songs, and we normally get through about fifty songs in four minutes! It's really fun.

MAX: I'm very excited because it's just us – just Max and Harvey. We're planning to perform, and then everyone will be able to meet us after the show. There will be a Q&A so the audience can ask questions too. It's going to be awesome.

ROYAL MANCHESTER CHILDREN'S HOSPITAL

HARVEY: We visited the children at Manchester Hospital today.

MAX: Our auntie's best friend's daughter had been treated there and they asked us to visit.

HARVEY: It was quite difficult to see so many people suffering from illness. And that's hard – not just for the child but also for the friends and family too. But the most amazing thing was that the kids we saw seemed very happy, even though some had been in hospital for a really long time. They were all upbeat people and they were so nice to talk to. Even with everything that's going on, they just get through it, and they don't see the bad side of things at all. It was quite humbling.

MAX: Yeah, that was definitely one of the harder experiences. Although everyone was jolly and happy, at the same time it was tough to see what they'd been going through. It was great to go there and try to cheer people up by singing for them. We were there to raise money for the ward, and we did so that was really cool. Two of the kids in the ward followed us on Musical.ly and it was great to meet them. One of them was a lovely girl who was really cheerful and very excited to see us, and we were just as excited to meet her. We just thought she was amazing. And we sang with her.

HARVEY: She was such a nice girl. All the people there were incredible – it was a really good thing to do. We're going to try to do it again – it's really fun, and if we can help out with fundraising a bit too, then that's awesome!

GRAVITY FORCE

HARVEY: We LOVE Gravity Force – it's a local trampoline park near where we live. We always go with our friends, and they asked us to host a night there.

MAX: It was different – we didn't actually perform – but it was still great. It was like going as we normally do, just to have fun with our mates, but then some of our fans were there too. So having fun but also sharing that experience with our fans was quite cool, and loads of people came.

HARVEY: It was, in a word, *mental*. We went with our three friends, and we took pictures with fans and signed photos and T-shirts and things like that. And we were also bouncing at the same time! It was a two-hour session, so not only did fans get to meet us but they also saw us very, very sweaty! I don't really know if that's a good thing or not – that's their decision, I guess!

MAX: Trampolining is one of our favourite things, so to do it with our friends *and* some people who follow us online was mad.

MARSHMELLO

MAX: We met Marshmello today! It was really cool because we'd been listening to his music for a while. When he approached us and said 'Would you like to meet?' we were, like, 'YES!' so we met him in London and did a few Musical.lys with him.

HARVEY: He was a really nice guy, and so was his manager. I love his helmet, and his music is so good – eveything is controlled through his phone! It's got thousands of different settings – it's just so colourful and amazing. It was great to talk to him.

MAX: He took a few shots for Instagram and it was fun and very random that he was in London! Obviously it wasn't that random for *him*, but we never expected it to happen.

HARVEY: It's really cool to meet people we follow online. We're going to VidCon in Amsterdam soon, and then to the Shorty Awards in New York – it's in the Easter holidays so our parents are letting us go! So we're really excited because we might get to meet more of the people we look up to.

MAX AND HARVEY'S LIST OF CELEBRITIES THEY WOULD MOST LIKE TO MEET

MAX:

1. Ariana Grande
2. Justin Bieber
3. Russell Howard
4. Michael McIntyre
5. Steve Carell
6. Jon Bellion
7. Daft Punk

HARVEY:

1. Logan Paul
2. Dynamo
3. Dave Franco
4. Ariana Grande
5. Eddie Redmayne
6. Ed Sheeran
7. James Corden
8. Ant and Dec
9. Derren Brown
10. Russell Howard

MAX AND HARVEY'S BEST (AND WORST) THINGS ABOUT BEING TWINS

MAX:

Best thing about Harvey:

He can sing quite well, I guess!

Worst thing about Harvey:

He knows a lot of ways to wind me up, and uses them against me!

HARVEY:

Best thing about Max:

Can play guitar well, I guess!

Worst thing about Max:

He thinks he's never wrong

Best thing about being twins:

1. Our voices work well together
2. You always have someone your own age to do things with
3. You can blame stuff on the other one!

SPRING

PERFORMING

MAX: We're getting really excited about the mini-tour we're doing in a few months – the Up Close tour – and we want it to be as awesome as possible. So we're practising loads and we've also just started working with a professional stage coach. He's teaching us about stage presence and how to use the stage. He gave us some cool ideas for our gigs.

HARVEY: It's getting us even more hyped up for the tour! His main tip was that we should move around more. When one of us is singing and one playing the guitar we used to just stand there, but now we're more organized – even though it's just walking around, no dance routines or anything! I love performing so it's great fun to do the rehearsals.

MAX: It gives me a thrill every time, and to hear a crowd cheering is insane. It requires a load of energy and we're always shattered afterwards, but it's totally worth it. As this is the first time it'll be just *our* show – not at a big event or anything – we want it to be really good, so we're doing a lot of practice in the evenings. We're busy at school as well so we're trying not to get too tired!

MAX AND HARVEY'S TOP TIPS FOR PERFORMING

MAX:

1. Channel any nervousness into energy and use it
2. Always keep the audience entertained
3. Always have a cool trick up your sleeve
4. If something goes wrong make sure you don't react in a bad way and try to find a way to make it right
5. Make sure you have fun!

HARVEY:

1. Be confident in yourself
2. Practise enough so you remember your set, but don't overdo it – it should be fun!
3. Don't worry about what people you don't know think – just listen to the opinion of people you trust.

SCHOOL

HARVEY: I still enjoy going to school. It is hard to balance with performing sometimes, but we're getting through it – we've just got to keep giving it our best. I want to continue doing both for as long as we can. Mum and Dad wouldn't let us do all our other stuff if it interfered with our schoolwork too much!

MAX: I've never had the passion for school that I have for performing – as you'd expect of pretty much every teenager! Though we're both still keeping up with the work, which is a surprise, considering we're going away, and practising for the tour, and making loads of videos, and trying to write songs. But it's still fun to be with our friends. I love lessons like music and drama.

HARVEY: When we did the *Sound of Music* UK tour last year, we were away from school quite a bit. We were set homework and had a tutor to help us with stuff. So even though we're really busy now, we should be able to keep up.

MAX: We missed our friends, but in some ways it's actually easier to learn with a tutor: there's just the two of us, and you can think about things a bit more. It takes up less time and you get more done. When you go to school, that's all you do for a whole day! What's good at school is that no one cares about our social media or singing or anything. We've had the same friends all the way through, and they don't care. Some teachers know, but I don't think they act any different. When they first find out, they're just a bit surprised by it – but that's all.

HARVEY: There are loads of great performers at our school. We just did *The Sound of Music* and it was really good! It was a lot of fun too. Everyone says it was one of the best shows the school has ever put on.

MAX: Everyone is really talented. It was interesting to see the differences between this production and the one we toured with last year. The directors had different interpretations, and we played different parts, but it went really well!

SUBJECTS

Max's favourite subjects:

1. Drama
2. PE
3. Geography
4. History
5. That's it! Oh, food tech. I like cooking.

Max's least favourite subjects:

1. ICT
2. Maths
3. English
4. French
5. Spanish

Harvey's favourite subjects:

1. Music
2. Drama
3. PE
4. History
5. Maths – just because of the teacher,
   I'm not good!

Harvey's least favourite subjects:

1. English
2. ICT
3. Science
4. Spanish
5. Design

DAILY ROUTINE

MAX: The other downside with school is that we don't get to hang out with the puppies! They're really healthy – they've all grown a lot.

HARVEY: They've almost all got homes lined up now. We've only had them for four weeks, but we've got to say goodbye soon.

MAX: A couple of days ago they went outside for the first time, which was quite funny – they just tumbled out into our garden. They're really cute. I don't want them to go. We're trying very hard to keep just one . . .

HARVEY: They're good for our videos! They've been on Musical.ly a lot!

MAX: We both love Musical.ly – it's our go-to app to do something if we need to.

HARVEY: Yes, it's a great way to get out there. There are ways in which it's changing, but it's still a really fun app.

MAX: We love talking to our fans on Musical.ly. One of the things they were asking was: *Do you have any merch?* We kind of thought, *No! We're not big enough to have merch!* But then we thought, *Why not?* So now we've started working on it.

HARVEY: Max and I went to meet this guy who specializes in merchandise stuff, and we drew what we wanted it to look like. We put the drawings together and digitized them and kept making changes, and now we've got a good design for the logo. We've chosen the colours too. I hope all the people who have been asking about it will like it.

MAX: We want it to be something *we* can wear too. If we choose to wear it, hopefully other people will too. That's not to say we have great fashion sense, but we're really excited about it. We can't wait to see if people like it. I hope it will be good . . .

HARVEY: Fingers crossed! We've actually got loads going on at the moment.

BBC UPDATE

HARVEY: We've just decided 100% to go ahead with the TV show for CBBC!

MAX: We just met the people who will actually be working on it – they are amazing.

HARVEY: Yeah, they came over to our house to talk about it. What makes me most excited is that we won't just be showing what we're doing music-wise: if we go out with our friends, for example, we'll probably film that so people can get to know us better than they do from social media. It'll be a lot of fun!

MAX: I'm so excited about the documentary – though I'm a bit nervous about things going wrong! Obviously I've never done a whole TV show where it's just based on me and Harvey – we don't know what to expect – but I can't wait.

HARVEY: I'm not worried at all! I don't like worrying about things before they've actually happened because that way you're living in the future. I just live in the moment: if there's a problem, I just let it

happen when it happens. I'm feeling really lucky to have all these opportunities: the show, the merch, songwriting – and soon we're going to VidCon in Amsterdam. I didn't really expect anything like this. It all just exploded out of nowhere on social media and I'm trying to enjoy every second of it.

MAX: I don't think I ever expected these opportunities either. When I was younger, I hoped I'd do something musical, but I never thought it would be anything like this. I thought I might do West End shows. But then we kind of got into this by mistake!

SONGWRITING

HARVEY: We've had a couple of songs written for us that we'll be performing at our next gig. We love hearing new songs. They are amazing! We love coming up with our own material too: it makes me proud to think, *I've just done that.*

MAX: We're still working with Metrophonic. They're really nice. It's weird to think we might write new stuff while we're working on this book! The dream is to release an album some day. We're writing lots of songs to show to record labels, and also so we can play more than just covers for our fans. Obviously that's a big dream and it might not happen, but we're having loads of fun trying!

MAX AND HARVEY'S SONGS THEY WISH THEY'D WRITTEN

MAX:

1. 'Stitches' by Shawn Mendez
2. 'All Time Low' by Jon Bellion
3. 'Counting Stars' by One Republic
4. 'Light It Up' by Major Lazer
5. 'Shape Of You' by Ed Sheeran
6. 'Galway Girl' by Ed Sheeran
7. '2U' by Justin Bieber
8. 'Scared To Be Lonely' by Dua Lipa and Martin Garrix
9. 'Something Just Like This' by The Chainsmokers and Coldplay

HARVEY:

1. 'You Need Me, I Don't Need You' by Ed Sheeran
2. 'Little Swing' by Aronchupa
3. 'Good Girls' by 5SOS
4. 'House Of Gold' by Twenty One Pilots
5. 'Migraine' by Twenty One Pilots

THE UP CLOSE TOUR – WARWICK

MAX: So we just had our first ever solo show in the UK!

HARVEY: It was so much fun! We went to Warwick and played at the Hilton. I think there were about 250 people. We couldn't believe so many showed up!

MAX: We wanted to perform and see our fans, but we had no idea how it would go down.

HARVEY: Everyone was really happy and everything went surprisingly well. Plus we sold merch there, which was fun.

MAX: It was a really well-run show! Not that I'm surprised, but the sound, lighting, stage – everything was great. We did a meet-and-greet with every single person there.

HARVEY: We've often met people who know us from social media – even out on the street – and we've done meet-and-greets at Gravity Force and places like that, but this was the first UK event that was just a Max and Harvey one.

MAX: There were a few different things for the performance: a meet-and-greet, where we had photos with everyone there, and a Q&A. Then we did our special chair drumming! (Trust me, it's not as weird as it sounds – if you haven't seen it, look it up!) Then there were two sets of about 20–25 minutes, and a 'four chord'.

HARVEY: It went really well, so we're going to announce two more shows, in London and Manchester, over half term.

WARWICK SET LIST:
'Stitches'
'No One Else'
'Closer'
'Counting Stars'
'Words'
'Migraine'
'Million Words'
'Sweet Lovin''
'One More Day'

VIDCON EU

MAX: It's the start of our Easter holidays, and we're at VidCon in Amsterdam. It's kind of chilled, but we're also working a bit. It's VidCon Europe: the first ever! We've got a few more trips coming up: after flying to New York for the Shorty Awards we're going to Orlando for Playlist Live. The whole family can't fly with us to America, so Mum, Dad, Leo and Tilly have all come to Amsterdam instead.

HARVEY: It's great to meet fans and see a new city, but also it's the first time we've actually met anyone from social media.

MAX: I met Saffron Barker, but at first I felt flustered – I didn't actually remember who she was! She came up to me and asked my name and what I do online and stuff. So I was like, 'I sing with my brother,' and she said, 'Oh, that's really cool, I'll see you another time,' and I said, 'Bye.' Then afterwards I told people, 'Someone named Saffron said hi to me,' and they just started going crazy! They kept saying, 'That's Saffron Barker – she's amazing!' And I was just like, 'Oh yeah!'

HARVEY: It was crazy – we met so many people: Amelia Gething, Houssein, Lisa and Lena, Tyler Oakley, TomSka. I'm a big fan of Jon Cozart's channel Paint, and we met him too. It was really cool to see what they're like in real life.

MAX: I've never been to Amsterdam before and I really like it – though no one told me that cyclists are a) everywhere, and b) so brutal. They don't stop for anyone, and neither do the trams! At least the trams ring a bell or something, but the cyclists just storm through. I nearly got hit several times!

HARVEY: It's a beautiful city to walk around – other than the road-safety thing! We're here for such a short time, but the flight is really short too, so that's OK. We're staying in a great apartment about twenty minutes away from VidCon – but actually I think a hotel would've been easier and nearer. It is still really nice though.

MAX: We've done two performances since we got here. Our first was on the main stage and we were in the Featured Creators show.

HARVEY: We had a sound check beforehand, and funnily enough it was just before Tyler Oakley's Q&A.

We effectively did the warm-up for his crowd! I know it sounds bad to say this, but I think the sound check went better than our show because there were a lot of people who wanted to see Tyler Oakley. When they saw us onstage, they were like, 'Oh, where's Tyler Oakley?' So we kept making jokes about Tyler Oakley not being there and they did find that funny. We were making them laugh because we were waiting for our tracks to work, and they were waiting for Tyler Oakley. So that was fun! Then, between the sound check and the gig, we went on the Musical.ly boat, and I inhaled helium, which I didn't realize at the time was really bad for my voice . . .

MAX: The first song went well – and then Harvey decided to lose his voice. So the second song was interesting . . . and by the end I realized that he couldn't even speak! I had to do all his bits for 'One More Day in Love', which was the final song. So the first performance was a bit of a mess. But he just had to look at me and I knew exactly what to do – I just sang his part. Maybe it's a twin thing!

HARVEY: My voice just kind of disintegrated. It wasn't even like I was losing my voice – it just wouldn't work. It was weird! I felt awful because the performance wasn't as good as it would have been and, me

being me, I was very upset. People probably hadn't even realized, but I just kept apologizing. It's kind of what I do. It was all right – I still think people enjoyed it and maybe they just felt bad.

MAX: The second performance on the Musical.ly stage was really good! We had a Q&A after, and Harvey did some magic, and we did some drumming on chairs that we flipped upside down. I played the guitar too.

HARVEY: Yes, my voice was fine by that time. We got a good reaction and everyone enjoyed it. So that made up for everything!

MAX: The weekend at VidCon was our first filming with the BBC, so maybe you'll get to see all that!

HARVEY: Yep, it was our first weekend working on the documentary. It was really interesting.

MAX: We met our crew for the first time, and they were all really nice! I think it's going to be brilliant making this show.

HARVEY: They already feel like a second family. We can't wait to film with them again! We expected everyone to be rushing around telling us what to do, but it's actually a lot of fun. You can see the camera, but you forget it's there. Sometimes we've actually started speaking to the crew rather than the camera, and they have to remind us that they're filming! Obviously, we have to watch what we say – that was a little worrying at first, but we soon got over it. Even if we say something bad, they can cut it! But the fact that it's being recorded is always a little intimidating: obviously, if you say something bad in real life and nobody records it, that's it, it's gone. But if someone is recording it, and you say something bad by accident, that doesn't always end well . . .

MAX: But we didn't feel nervous. We've been filmed before, though we've never walked around with cameras following our every move – so that was a bit different!

THE SHORTY AWARDS

MAX: On Wednesday we flew out to New York City!

HARVEY: We were nominated for Muser of the Year so we've come to NYC for the awards ceremony. Unfortunately we didn't win – Lisa and Lena won – but we still had an awesome time.

MAX: It was our first ever nomination for any type of award so it was an amazing experience and really cool to be in New York.

HARVEY: We got to meet loads of American social media stars too. The Perkins Sisters were really nice. We did a couple of interviews with them, for *Backstage* magazine and *Teen Vogue*.

MAX: We were with Zach Clayton (BruhitsZach), who won the award for YouNower of the Year. It was an amazing night, with loads going on everywhere.

HARVEY: We went to an after party and met a lot of cool people like Thomas Sanders, who is on Vine. He was a really nice guy. And we also met Collins Key,

who was on *America's Got Talent*. It was all awesome but so, so busy. We had to leave because we were so hungry. We ended up going to the Hard Rock Café.

MAX: We met Zach Clayton because we've been asked to go on tour with him in a few months. We went to his hotel and we thought, *Hey, let's make a YouTube video!* And we went out to get the Unicorn Frappuccino they had in Starbucks in America for one weekend only and make a video of it.

HARVEY: But they'd sold out everywhere, which really upset me! Apparently it was horrible, but I really wanted to try it for myself.

MAX: So we ended up not making a YouTube video. That was our first ever time meeting Zach: scurrying around New York trying to find that Unicorn drink and coming back empty-handed!

HARVEY: We also went to see *Kinky Boots* on Broadway. I didn't expect to like it much, but it was incredibly good.

MAX: It was really cold in New York – even colder than in England. But it was really great to be there again. We've only been once before.

HARVEY: We made something for Musical.ly that went horribly wrong! There's a YouTube video up about it. We did this challenge – going around Central Park in a bunny costume, but we couldn't find a bunny costume! So we ended up getting a bear costume and a penguin costume and wandering around the park, photo-bombing, joining in with people's yoga classes, stuff like that. It was a bit weird . . .

MAX: I really like New York, but I can't imagine myself actually living here – a) because it's very cold, and b) because the smell isn't so great! But other than that, it's awesome.

HARVEY: If I lived here, I'd probably never sleep! Most nights I didn't get much sleep anyway because we got in late, but I can't imagine what it would be like if I lived here. It's so mental. It's such an amazing place, but, yeah, I can't imagine living here – it would be too tiring!

MAX AND HARVEY'S THINGS THEY LOVE ABOUT FANS

MAX:

1. They are crazy (in a good way)
2. They are so supportive of everything we do
3. They are all amazing
4. They are very loud! Which is good!

HARVEY:

1. They're so enthusiastic and loud
2. They put so much effort into everything they do
3. They're extremely loyal
4. They're all really nice
5. They're the coolest people out there!

TRAVEL

MAX: I love flying. The only thing that scares me is when it gets a bit turbulent, but it's usually fine! And so worth it when you get where you're going.

HARVEY: I love America. We've been to Florida, LA and New York so far, and we have lots of stops on the Zach Clayton tour. I want to visit as many places as possible. I love to travel to different places and experience other cultures.

MAX AND HARVEY'S TRAVEL WISH LIST . . .

MAX:

1. Hawaii
2. LA (I'd love to live there)
3. Tokyo
4. Australia
5. Brazil
6. Canada
7. Beijing
8. Texas
9. Spain

HARVEY:

1. Dubai
2. South Africa
3. Australia (we went when we were two years old but I can't remember any of it)
4. Las Vegas
5. Canada

PUPDATE

MAX: The puppies are now nine weeks old – so they're big enough to be taken home by their new families. Saying goodbye was very sad.

HARVEY: We'll miss them a lot. After all, they're puppies! Who wouldn't hate saying goodbye to puppies?!

MAX: Luckily we didn't actually have to see them go – we were in New York when most of the new owners came to collect them, so we said goodbye before we left. When we got back there were only two left – a boy and a girl. The last girl was picked up the day after we got home.

HARVEY: I'm glad we were away. I knew they were going but I didn't have to watch them leave. But the good news is, we get to keep one! So we have kept Pumba, who we've renamed Freddie.

MAX: He's awesome. The only trouble is, he chews cables. Cables are his favourite toy, so we have to watch out for that. He could choose to chew on

FREDDIE

pillows or anything else, and that probably wouldn't bother us as much. But no, he had to choose cables! It was pretty bad until we trained him not to.

HARVEY: He's a little terror! He chewed through a really expensive pair of headphones. He's not properly trained yet – he just goes to the toilet wherever he happens to be . . . which isn't very pleasant. We're working on it – he should be fine within the next few weeks. Hopefully he'll be a bit better behaved too.

MAX: Pippa gets quite annoyed with him. They fight all the time – though it's play-fighting. He bites Pippa's ears and jumps on top of her, so it's understandable that she gets a bit fed up. But, you know, they'll get along some day.

HARVEY: Freddie is super cute, so he gets away with it!

PLAYLIST

MAX: Harvey and I were so excited to go to Playlist! Playlist Live is a convention in Orlando, Florida, for social media stars and artists who have a big following.

HARVEY: The set-up is amazing. It's an event similar to VidCon, where all the creatives and influencers are gathered together. There are performances and meet-and-greets where fans get to see them in person.

MAX: We flew out to Orlando with our mum. When we got to the hotel, I thought we'd have to get in a car and drive to Playlist. But, no, it was actually *in* the hotel, which was insanely massive. It held about 15,000 people! It was so big there was a North, East, West and South Tower. The East and South were for fans and the North was for influencers, and they were very, very strict about it. If you didn't have a certain key card, you weren't allowed through. At the start we didn't have that key card because we got there early, and the people at reception didn't give us one, which was a bit stressful! As soon as we had the cards it was a lot easier – I saw so many fans trying to get in . . .

HARVEY: The fans there were just amazing. It was hard to walk around without being stopped.

MAX: If we were walking from one place to another, it took us about half an hour because there were so many people everywhere. It was really nice to meet them.

HARVEY: Yeah, it was fun. And obviously, the first thing people said to us was: 'I love your accent.' And on the Sunday night they closed down Universal Studios Park so that anyone who was part of Playlist could go there.

MAX: We got to go on rides with all our new friends, and we didn't have to queue for more than five minutes! We went on as many as we could.

HARVEY: We were with HRVY, Loren Gray, Danielle Cohn, Bryce Xavier, Blake Gray, Baby Ariel, Christian Lalama, Amelia Gething and Houssein. We also met JoJo Siwa – she was really friendly and she spent the whole weekend at the Musical.ly stage.

MAX: One of the funniest people I met there was Jackson Anderson. I'd never seen him before, but he was hilarious. I met Tanner Braungardt too. He creates amazing videos. We went to IHOP and he was really interesting.

HARVEY: We also did some live performances and meet-and-greets, like we did at VidCon Europe.

MAX: All our performances went pretty well except one . . . We were doing a couple of shows that day, and during the first one I noticed that something was wrong with my voice – it cracked a couple of times. But in our second performance it just went. When that happened to Harvey at VidCon Europe, I just stepped in to sing his bits, and I was kind of counting on him to do the same for me. But I don't think he heard it – he was off doing his own thing, and I was trying to let him know I couldn't sing at all! He didn't quite get the message . . .

ZACH CLAYTON TOUR

HARVEY: Straight after Playlist we went to Chicago to meet up with Zach Clayton. We were supporting him on the Nothin' But Love tour. We'd been looking forward to it for ages so we couldn't wait to start!

MAX: It was amazing. It was our first ever proper tour in America and it was just awesome to meet US fans. Now we're friends with Zach and Sanni, who is on the tour too, so it's great that we did the tour. And we saw loads of new places. We flew from Playlist in Orlando to Chicago, because it's a long way. The second leg of the tour was in Cleveland, and we drove in a van, which actually only took about four or five hours. But then the third venue was in Brooklyn, New York – that took about eight hours – and then Brooklyn to Boston for the last night took about five hours as well. So, yeah, very long trips, but it was fun being on the road.

CHICAGO

CLEVELAND

Met up with Zach in Chicago and played the first show of the tour. Went to a trampoline park after the show.

Drove from Chicago to Cleveland in a van! Played show in Cleveland.

Caught the plane to Chicago after playing at Playlist Live in Orlando.

ORLANDO

CANADA

 SPRING

Drove from Cleveland to Brooklyn, New York
for the next show. Discovered Popeyes fried
chicken on the way.

BOSTON

NEW YORK

Went to Times
Square after the
show. Ate
Caramel M&Ms!

Drove from Brooklyn to
our last show in Boston.
Had some amazing
pancakes!

THE USA

HARVEY: Yeah, there were a couple of rough nights, I have to admit, but we got through them! Most of the time we got to sleep in nice hotels, but sometimes we were just sleeping in the van – we loved it though.

MAX: In Chicago we stayed in quite an old-fashioned hotel. As soon as we got there we put our stuff down and went out – and a fan found us in the corridor because they were staying in the same hotel. We'd obviously met loads of fans at Playlist, but they were there to see other people as well. So that was cool. We just took a few pictures, spoke to them for a while, and then we headed straight for a trampoline park – we love trampoline parks! The Chicago show was insane – an awesome first show. It was in a studio so the stage had to be brought in and set up, but it was good to perform in. The sound was great, the audience was great – the whole thing was just so much fun.

HARVEY: This is how the set worked: obviously Zach was the headliner, Sanni was the opening act (except for the Boston show, when we were because we had to leave early to catch our plane home). Then we were effectively the support act. We played around five songs – roughly the same number as Zach – as well as doing our drumming routine. Usually we sang 'Migraine' by Twenty One Pilots, which worked well because there's a one-word response after each line so we got the crowd to do it. That was really cool because they were just so loud! We posted that on Musical.ly as well. We did our original songs 'One More Day in Love' and 'No One Else'.

MAX: After Chicago we drove to Cleveland. We had a day to relax . . . but instead of relaxing, we went to another trampoline park – probably one of the best I've been to. But the really weird thing was that the people working there recognized us. It was so strange to be in a random trampoline park in Ohio and have people notice us . . . but we got an extra half-hour on the trampolines because of it, so that was good! Although I did cut my shoulder – which was already sunburned from Florida – on a door, and when it came to hugging fans the next day, that was a bit painful . . .

HARVEY: The show in Cleveland was one of the best, I reckon.

MAX: The room was slightly smaller than the other venues so it looked really full. It was completely packed, and everyone was a lot louder. It was an amazing show. My shoulders killed, but I didn't really care. We introduced a new thing where we go on in animal costumes for the first number. We just thought, *Hey, we've got a penguin suit and a bear suit from New York – why don't we use them?* So we did, and now, for the first number, we're going to wear animal costumes.

HARVEY: Then we drove on to New York. There was one great thing that Zach introduced me to on the tour: Popeyes. We tried it, and then I ordered it at least three more times while we were there. It's probably one of my favourite fast-food places now – especially the chicken wings. That was the up side of being on the road, definitely.

MAX: So the third show was in Brooklyn. It was at a venue called the Knitting Factory, which you might think would be quite calm – but no. It was a full-on club where bands play. During the day we chilled out in New York, and then we had another great performance. Everyone was really loud. We enjoyed meeting all the fans, and, yeah, it was really fun. After the show we went to Times Square with Zach and Sanni, and bought caramel M&Ms because they're new. They taste really weird, but good. I don't like M&Ms, but I like the caramel ones. I think Americans have better candy but the UK have better chocolate. I think that's what it is.

HARVEY: We went back to the hotel, where we attempted (and note the word *attempted*) to make slime for a YouTube video . . . and it's a lot harder than you might think. Especially when you haven't got anything to measure everything out with. It was extremely difficult and horrible and messy. The closest we got was probably Max's; his was all right. We tried every possible kind of mixture and technique and it just didn't work at all. The day we made the video we were due to leave, which was awkward because the bathroom was covered in slime . . . There's really no normal way of explaining how that happened!

MAX: After that we drove to Boston for the last show of the tour. In the morning we went to eat at International House of Pancakes (IHOP). It was really good. We've been there at least seven times since we came to America. We love it!!

HARVEY: That evening we were on first, and then we had to jump in a taxi to the airport to fly home – we couldn't even wait to see the others. It was sad!

MAX: We had such an awesome time. Touring in the US is definitely a lot different to the UK. In the US, not gonna lie, they're very crazy – but good crazy. Definitely good crazy. But it was just an insane experience. So is being in Britain, but it's our home turf. It was great to see how another country reacts to what we do.

HARVEY: It was nice because Americans are different from people in the UK. I can't really say what it is . . . I think British people can actually be louder, but the Americans have got a great energy. It was so cool touring over there, and we got to see some places we'd never visited before. And the people who came to see us were so generous too! It was lovely to meet them.

MAX: Although . . . there was one weird thing. We had just finished our final show in Boston and were off to the airport. As we walked out of the venue there was a girl of about twelve with her mum and we stopped to say hello. Then the mum said, 'Can my daughter have your T-shirts?' We said, 'You mean the T-shirts that we're wearing?' and she said, 'Yeah, she wants them as a memento.' We were just about to go to the airport and get on a plane – we'd be half naked! It was just really weird and kind of awkward. We just had to apologize and say no . . . They were fine with it – but it was very odd!

HARVEY: The main thing I got was tape. In a YouTube video once, we were using tape and I decided to wrap my face up in it (DON'T try this at home, guys!) – and then that kind of became a thing on Instagram. And now, every time a fan gives me tape I'll just wrap myself in it and post it somewhere. This was a big part of the Nothin' But Love tour: we decided to wrap my whole body in tape and actually posted a couple of videos on Musical.ly. It was quite funny, but the first time I didn't prepare well for it – I had no sleeves, and when we took off the tape there were horrible marks on my arms. All in the name of art!

MAX: I'm excited to be going home now, even though I'm sad the tour's over. I definitely missed my bed! And of course I missed my family, I missed the puppy and Pippa, and even my old cat Minnie, who is (in a nice way) somehow still alive. I missed loads of things at home. But then, all our new friends were so nice: they know what it's like to have this sort of platform, and sometimes it's good to hang out with people who get what we're doing. We're hoping to return to the States in August. Still, it's great to go back to normal and be with our school friends again. The only thing is – we have exams . . .

BACK TO SCHOOL

HARVEY: Here's a little-known fact about Max and me: we can't sleep on planes. We just can't do it. The flight was an overnight one, and we landed in the morning, UK time. So we didn't sleep, and we were awake for about 36 hours. Then . . . we went to bed that night and had to go to school the next day.

MAX: I feel quite bad. While we were in America we missed our end-of-year exams . . . And today, on the first day back, I had an English exam first thing in the morning, which was the worst.

HARVEY: We did study a lot while we were away. Our mum was with us and we did a couple of hours almost every day. While we were on the road we were mainly revising, but also doing the homework that everyone got set anyway so we didn't fall behind. And now all my friends have finished their exams, but I've still got, like, five to do. So I'm a little bit behind but I'll be fine!

MAX: I still feel jet-lagged, which is not very nice. I don't know about anyone else, but I can be a bit grumpy when I'm tired. It was OK – I didn't do anything bad or fall asleep in the middle of class. It was just readjusting to school life and all that kind of stuff. And it was obviously worth it to go to Playlist and tour in America. We get to do both fun stuff *and* school!

HARVEY: Obviously being away makes it a little more difficult because you don't actually have a teacher. But we got through all the work by ourselves and everything seemed OK. We'll see what our results are like . . . I'm not that stressed out about it because I pick things up quickly when I really focus . . . I hope!

MAX: Except for me being just terrible at science, I think things at school and what we're doing at the moment are working really well. But, yeah, it was tough going back and having to do a load of exams right after the trip to America. We were prepared for it, but it was kind of tiring.

HARVEY: I was really out of it at school and just trying my hardest to seem alive. Now we've got one more week, and then it's a half term, and then we're going to do the second two Up Close shows. The three months between now and the end of summer are horribly busy, but we always knew that they would be. It's also really fun. We want to make the most of every opportunity. Today just felt tiring. It's gonna be interesting.

SUPERFAN

MAX: Today at school a very weird thing happened.

HARVEY: This girl – I think she was from Germany – must have found out where we go to school and she called us there. Apparently she rang reception and said, 'Hi, can I speak to Max and Harvey please?'

MAX: The receptionist had to say, 'No, sorry, we can't do that. They're in lessons and they're not allowed to speak to you – we don't know who you are.' So the call ended, and then a friend of our mum's who works at the school called us and said, 'These girls called in at the school asking for Max and Harvey today.'

HARVEY: I found it quite funny when we got the message that someone had called the school asking to talk to us. It's obviously really nice of them to be fans of ours, but we're also just normal kids at school – I don't want to sound ungrateful, but I do think it's a little weird.

MAX: And then, after school, when I was walking to my friend's house, these German girls just came up to me out of nowhere. I guess they must be the same girls. They asked for a picture, and of course I said, 'Yep, that's fine.' But I was kind of freaked out at the same time. It's the first time that's happened to us. We've obviously met lots of people before, but no one's tried to find out where we live or go to school or anything like that. It was kind of scary.

THE UP CLOSE TOUR – MANCHESTER

HARVEY: On Friday, straight after we broke up for half term, we drove up to Manchester with our dad and stayed in a hotel. We were with the CBBC crew all weekend too.

MAX: Playing in Manchester this week was obviously very difficult, because the terrorist attack at the Ariana Grande concert had only happened the weekend before. A couple of people didn't show up, which was understandable, though it was a shame not to have them there. We decided not to cancel the show: we love Manchester and everyone was so brave. We didn't want to let people down, and anyone who felt scared could obviously choose not to come – we totally got that.

HARVEY: The gig went really well – though unfortunately the fire alarm went off in the middle and, coming so soon after the attack, it was quite scary. Max and I tried to keep as calm as we could, but there were quite a few people crying and screaming. Everyone was OK – it was only because of someone smoking. But it was pretty creepy.

MAX: Yeah, in the middle of the Q&A a fire alarm went off and we looked at our sound person and asked if it was a joke – which would have been really not funny, obviously – and she said 'No.' So we told the crowd, and everyone was out of the building in, like, two minutes. The security team were amazing – they got people out so quickly.

HARVEY: Everyone was crying and quite upset. We were all just standing out in the street. But then we found out it was just someone smoking on the top floor. We felt bad that people had been so scared. But once it was sorted they were all very understanding and managed to forget what happened.

MAX: We went back into the room and carried on with the show and it was completely fine. Everything went well after that.

HARVEY: We continued where we'd left off. We finished our Q&A session, and then we had a little break before the second set so everyone could calm down. After that it was great. But it was so sad that this happened during the week of the Manchester attack. I'm so glad we got to carry on with the show – I hope people had a really good time.

THE GREAT MANCHESTER RUN

HARVEY: It was probably a few months ago now that we did our first mini-campaign for the Royal Manchester Children's Hospital. Our auntie originally spoke to us about Ward 84, which is the cancer ward. Her friend's daughter was there and the staff were just amazing, so our auntie and her friends were trying to spread the word and raise money for it. That's when we did our first online campaign for them, and we've also been in to meet people. It's just kind of grown out of that – it's incredible how many people are doing stuff for it, even just sending love online. On the Sunday after our gig in Manchester it was the Great Manchester Run and people were running for charities like the Royal Manchester Children's Hospital.

MAX: We got to blow these air horns for the start of the race and perform for the runners in the kids' races when they crossed the finish line. We met the most amazing little girl who ran in the youngest race – she must have been about five. She was running with a support because of her illness. Right at the end of the race she just dropped it and sprinted for the finish – it was the most incredible thing.

HARVEY: Yeah, it was inspiring to see how many young people were running for these charities. Some of the kids were so fast. I think the older children ran 2.5 kilometres and one of them did it in, like, eight minutes. It was ridiculous. I thought we would have a lot more time before they reached the finish line. Suddenly this kid comes round the corner, and then there was quite a big gap before the next one. A few finished in under twelve minutes, and the rest took about fifteen or twenty, which is still amazing. The five- to nine-year-olds ran one kilometre. Some of them did it in around fifteen minutes, which was insane! It was really cool to see.

MAX: It was such a fun day. We did a few interviews. We actually used in-ear systems to hear ourselves on the track, which was a first. And a loud first, as well! I don't think we had the volume setting quite right – I heard myself a bit too loudly! The crowd were moving around a lot, because obviously everyone was running. But it was still one of the biggest crowds

95

we've played to – around 1,500. Luckily I don't think we've ever been properly nervous about anything. I mean, I always get butterflies before I go on stage – I love the fact that I'm about to perform for a lot of people. I think the only time I've ever been like 'Ooh, what if something goes wrong?' is when we did a fireworks show in our home town last November and there were thousands of people there. That hit me cos it was a big performance for us quite early on. But today's was one of the most rewarding we've done. The kids there are just so great. It was a brilliant experience and everything went really well. It was awesome.

HARVEY: Unfortunately we didn't take part in the race because we were performing while people were running. I would've loved to, even though – believe me – I cannot run. Actually, when we got there, Tilly really wanted to run take part, but unfortunately you had to sign up online or something and get your number and all that. So it was too late . . . She wasn't really dressed for it either!

Hanging out with Leo and Tilly in Amsterdam at VidCon EU

At the Shorty Awards! ▲

◀ *Meeting Doug the Pug!*

Puppies, puppies, PUPPIES! ▲

Pippa and Freddie ▼

At a wax museum in Florida ▲

More waxworks . . . ▶

At a Blue Man Group show in Florida ▲

Be Seen in Green in Manchester ▼

Kicking off the Zach Clayton tour in style ▲

BTS photo shoot ▶

The Instagram area at VidCon

Arriving at VidCon in Anaheim ▶

▲ Busking at Camp Bestival – last year
(much less muddy!)

Performing for
3,000 people at
Camp Bestival
this year! ▶

'BE SEEN IN GREEN'

MAX: The Royal Manchester Children's Hospital asked us to write a song for primary schools to sing in assemblies and things. So we said, 'Yeah, we can definitely do that.' Our mum helped us write the song and I worked out the music and all that kind of stuff. We recorded it, got it mastered, and it ended up sounding better than I expected. It's a really nice song for children to sing, and it raises awareness about the work of the hospital. It's called 'Be Seen in Green'.

HARVEY: We really wanted to help support the Royal Manchester Children's Hospital – it's important to our family because of our auntie's friend's daughter. She was only about three or four when she went through chemotherapy there. They did an amazing job supporting her. And they work so hard: when we went to meet all the kids there were just people everywhere making sure that everyone was OK.

MAX: At the moment Harvey and I don't do much songwriting because we have so little time after school, and then as soon as we get home, we're normally doing things like chores and homework or getting all of the Musical.lys done, or posting a photo for Instagram. And sometimes, we'll be asked by record companies to learn a song and we try to fit in live streams because we enjoy that so much. Then we'll have dinner as a family, and after that our parents make sure we do something to relax, so we do something fun like watch the TV with our mum and dad before we go to sleep. So we're very busy at the moment. Songwriting is very minimal, but we really wanted to do this when we were asked, and Mum helped out.

HARVEY: Mum is actually very good at writing songs for kids. She wrote a song when we were leaving our primary school, and that went down really well – they've used it for the past four years now. We're not charging for 'Be Seen in Green' or anything – we just want to spread awareness of the charity. The song's on SoundCloud, so people can download and listen to it. It's spreading already, which is so cool. There have been quite a few videos on Instagram and Musical.ly. One group of girls spent a long time making a music video to it, and it was really cool, so we posted it on our Instagram. It's great to see how much effort people put into these things.

MAX: Yeah – it was awesome. And tons of people are supporting the charity. It's worked really, really well in terms of raising awareness.

HARVEY: We've also set a little challenge: people either sing along to the song or make a video to it online. 'Be Seen in Green' is going to be sent to lots of primary schools around Manchester. If they like it they can enter a competition for us to come and sing in one of their assemblies after we're back from VidCon. So hopefully some people will enter, because that would be fun! I think we'll try to make a day of it and visit the children on the ward as well.

LYRICS:

It can happen in a moment
Everything can change
All of the things you knew
Can suddenly rearrange
Find a new horizon
Something different than before
Look further than you thought you could
And you will find an open door

Music makes the world sound better
It can brighten up your day
Music makes the world seem brighter
It can help in many ways
Music makes the world sound better
It can brighten up your day
Music makes the world seem brighter
It can help in many ways

Be seen in green
Yeah yeah
Be seen in green
Show the world you can be seen in
   green

It's easy to be frightened
Of a world with wonders new
But if you look around and see
It just comes down to being you
Look through all of your dreams
Grab hold and really try
This is your new story
So take up your wings and fly

Music makes the world sound better
It can brighten up your day
Music makes the world seem brighter
It can help in many ways
Music makes the world sound better
It can brighten up your day
Music makes the world seem brighter
It can help in many ways

Chorus

Music makes the world sound better
It can brighten up your day
Music makes the world seem brighter
It can help in many ways
Music makes the world sound better
It can brighten up your day
Music makes the world seem brighter
It can help in many ways

Chorus x 2

UP CLOSE TOUR – LONDON

HARVEY: When we got back from Manchester we had a really fun half term hanging out with our friends – because we've been so busy with going to Playlist and touring and then exams it was really nice to chill. And on the final day of the holiday we had our last Up Close gig in London, which was amazing!

MAX: Yeah, it was so, so good. We had the really cool merch that we've had for the whole tour. We had caps with our logo, lanyards, stickers and two different colour T-shirts: one blue, one maroon – our favourite colours.

HARVEY: We wanted people (and us!) to have something to remember it by. I mean hopefully they'd remember it anyway! But having something to look at and think, *Oh, I remember this happening* helps. We are working on getting more merch now; we're working on PopSockets and we're hoping to get hoodies as well.

MAX: The show was the same as the other ones in terms of what we performed, but the crowd was amazing and it was kind of special because it was our last Up Close show.

HARVEY: And there were no fire alarms this time, which was good!

BACK TO SCHOOL AGAIN

HARVEY: We're back again, after a really fun half term!

MAX: The good news is that this last part of the school year won't be so bad because we've done all our tests. Turns out we did well in most of them. I can't say I did brilliantly in science, but you know, it's science. It's not my strongest. I did well in maths and English, which I was happy about. And then all the other subjects I did OK in. So I don't think we missed out on anything by being on tour. Except for me being just terrible at science. Nothing could have changed that.

HARVEY: Actually, my best result was probably in history. If it was GCSE my teacher said I would've got an A for it. Probably the worst one was the harder maths exam, where I did pretty horribly. There was a normal maths exam but there was also a harder one that only two classes took. And I was pretty bad at it. I mean, I didn't get the worst mark, but I didn't get the best at all.

. . . AND EXAM RESULTS

MAX: I think we're balancing school with our other stuff really well at the moment. We're not getting bad grades or anything. So yeah, even though it was tough thinking, *Right, after this trip to America we're gonna go back and have to do a load of exams*, it was fine. And we're off to LA for VidCon next week, which is so exciting.

HARVEY: We're not missing anything major while we're away, and we'll be doing homework as usual. Well, except for sports day, but I'm pretty poor at sport. I couldn't run even if there was something chasing me, I'd probably just fall. I'll stick to singing. That's probably a better option for me. Who needs sport? I mean, obviously people enjoy it. But it's not for me!

WE ♥ OUR FOLLOWERS

HARVEY: We hit 500,000 followers on Instagram!

MAX: We are SO excited! A couple of months ago we weren't expecting to hit 500,000 at all. But before we went to Playlist we were on about 310,000, and by the time we left America we had nearly hit 400,000. And we were like, 'Wow, that went up quite quickly!' We were surprised, and then it just kept building and building so fast. We were quite weirded out by it, but we weren't complaining! We love that we hit 500,000 and we are hopefully going to do a YouTube video or something like that. We are very happy.

HARVEY: Maybe one day we'll get to a million . . . and then we'll do something crazy. We're trying to think of something cool to mark it because we also hit four million followers on Musical.ly recently. We were thinking of doing something with Amelia Gething and Houssein – it would be nice, because they're also British musers and we've become really good friends. And we'll see them at VidCon soon.

MAX: Yeah! Four million on Musical.ly was really exciting. We can't wait to hopefully hit five, then ten, then 500,000 million! It's just a growing process on Musical.ly and we love everyone who supports us, follows us and shares our videos to bring in new fans to the family. The range of people who are interested in what we do has changed so fast. Before, it was just like distant aunts and a few family members who liked what we did, and now it's close to four million people!

HARVEY: Some people we've met at conventions seem to think of Musical.ly as a job, but we don't – we just love making music, and Musical.ly is for fun. We can also use it as a vlogging tool to keep in touch with our fans. It's cool to keep people excited about what we're doing. I like sharing lots of things with our fans. It sounds cringey, but it really *is* like a big family! We appreciate everything people do for us so much.

SUMMER

VIDCON USA

MAX: We are SO EXCITED about VidCon USA!

HARVEY: I really think it's going to be amazing – apparently it's even crazier than Playlist.

MAX: We flew out to California today, Sunday – three days before the convention starts. We get to go as Featured Creators, and all the Featured Creators are put in the same hotel – so we get to be with loads of YouTubers and people we really look up to. It's so awesome. We're only about three minutes from the convention centre.

HARVEY: We're here with Mum as Dad has to work and look after Tilly and Leo. Next time we go to the USA, in the summer holidays, they're all going to come but it was just not possible this time.

MAX: It's really hot so we've just dumped our stuff in our room and we're heading down to the pool. We're keeping a diary while we're here so we'll always remember it and can share it with you guys . . .

MONDAY

MAX: Today we went shopping – Mum wanted to go to Target, and it is also Zach's birthday tomorrow. We've been invited to his party on Wednesday so we went to get him some presents. We got him a bag with a unicorn and a rainbow on it and inside it we put glue, Jell-O, sunglasses and English chocolate. Thoughtful gifts – not at all random!

HARVEY: We mainly just hung out with Mum and got used to the time difference. It's really sunny here. We're doing a Max and Harvey gig tomorrow night. We haven't had much time to organize it but we really want to perform as much as possible while we're here, so we'll see how that goes! We've been doing a bit of rehearsing, but we're going to use the Up Close tour set-list, which we know really well by now.

HARVEY: We had lunch at the Cheesecake Factory, which was so good. Cassie and Mika came to meet us in Anaheim – they're going to be at VidCon too. It was really nice to see them!

MAX: Then we did our first ever Max and Harvey headliner show in America. We had a crowd of about 120 people – probably about half what we get in the UK. It was very short notice so we were just really happy that anyone came. It was great to see them all. It was in a place called Chain Reaction in Anaheim.

HARVEY: It went great. It felt different to the Zach Clayton tour as people were there to see us, which was so nice. Christian Lalama supported us and he was amazing. We were very happy to have him there. And the crowd were brilliant – really loud and fun.

MAX: I really enjoyed it – I hope we can do more solo shows this summer! That's the dream, anyway. It's so great to be here! It's sort of how I felt at Playlist: I miss school and home, obviously, but it is so cool to be around loads of people doing the same thing as us. It's fun.

WEDNESDAY

HARVEY: Today we recorded with Mika in a studio here in Anaheim. It was a brand-new song called 'Chemistry'. I really like it. There's another called 'Stuck on the Ceiling', which I think I actually prefer, but we didn't have time to record that too.

MAX: And then in the evening we went to Zach's party where we saw him for the first time since his tour.

HARVEY: It was at a bowling alley and so many YouTubers and friends of ours were there. We gave Zach his presents. I think he liked them . . . !

MAX: We knew everyone from Playlist – it was fun to see them again. Then we went to IHOP. We love IHOP, as you've definitely heard already in this book!

HARVEY: Then we went on to a party that YouTube hosted for everyone who was a Featured Creator at VidCon. It was at a go-karting place and we went with loads of people from Zach's party. There was this random electric drum kit outside and no one was playing it – so I asked the DJ if I could. He said yes, so I played for half an hour and now I've got such a bad blister!

THURSDAY

HARVEY: The start of VidCon!

MAX: The very first thing we did was go to the What's Trending stage and do an interview – one of the most fun interviews ever. Most of the time you just sit at a table but this was in front of a live audience.

HARVEY: Yep, and we sang a couple of songs. Then we went on to the Musical.ly stage, which we are hosting for about half the weekend.

MAX: We were hosting with Jess Flores. She helped us out as we'd never hosted a stage before! We really enjoyed it – which is lucky, because we spent the whole day there today! We were there from about 10 a.m. to 5.30 p.m. It was a very long day but it was fun. It was interesting to see the crowds different people attract. This is how it worked: we were there all day introducing people, and sometimes we performed too, but mainly we were presenting and saying who was on next and things. It was great to watch all the acts; there are some really talented people on Musical.ly. It doesn't matter how many followers you have online – the people who are most talented get the biggest crowds in real life!

HARVEY: In our break we went to the Instagram area. We walked around VidCon wearing chicken and alpaca masks – we got bigger crowds than we would have done if people had seen our faces, I think! And we were in the Instagram story. There was a massive hamster wheel in their area and we ran on it. You can see that on our Instagram – it was pretty cool!

MAX: We were escorted everywhere by security, which was a bit weird. But it wasn't too bad for us – it was much worse for more famous people; some of them weren't allowed to walk around at all! If we needed to go anywhere we had to have an escort. It was cool though – like walking around with a superhero! But sometimes they were a bit mean to people! It made us look like divas: everywhere we went we were flanked by guys shoving people out of the way. Some of them were huge, like three times my size! We still got to meet loads of fans and stuff. And so many people gave us fidget spinners!

HARVEY: We hosted the Musical.ly stage again today. We started first thing, then we had a two-hour break, and then we carried on until everything started to close. I went to get something to eat at the Hilton, which is where Amelia and Houssein were staying. But Mum texted me to say I had to come back. And then, two minutes after I left, Logan Paul showed up! I'm a massive Logan Paul fan – I was so annoyed. But when we were on stage we heard screams outside and we found out that it was him getting mobbed by thousands of fans! It was insane. He thought there would be about a hundred people outside, but there were thousands! I recommend the video – it's crazy. So cool. One person tweeted him saying they got their food knocked out of their hand – I feel sorry for them! I hate dropping food. And obviously I feel bad for the security guards. But it was mental.

MAX: Logan Paul had hidden $3,000 at VidCon and posted a set of clues on social media. When he went to give the money to the person who found it, he got trapped in a fountain – by thousands of fans! He jumped in to try to get away and they just followed him. He had to sprint away to his hotel! It was quite funny to watch but really terrifying too . . .

HARVEY: Yes – suddenly it doesn't seem so bad having security walk us around! In the evening they closed the convention centre for a bit and then reopened it just for Featured Creators, so the really famous people could walk around without getting mobbed by fans. We got slimed on the Nickleodeon stand! I always wanted to do that – we did it with JoJo Siwa – she didn't want to but we did. It was so nice to spend time with our social media friends.

MAX: I got slimed, and played hot wheels, and made doughnuts. It was a great night – what more could you want!

HARVEY: The slime was surprisingly warm! Also, there was a Calvin Klein lounge where they were giving out free stuff. That was pretty cool. Max and Mum had an argument over a jacket – he ordered one and she forgot to pick it up. I thought it was funny. Oh, and we stole about a hundred packets of Orbeez. We're going to try to make a video with them tomorrow.

MAX: I think tonight was my favourite part of the whole week so far! The Perkins Sisters, Amelia Gething, Houssein and Jackson Anderson were there. It was great to hang out with them again after Playlist. Plus some big names – Roman Atwood, Colleen Ballinger aka Miranda Sings (she was so nice!), JoJo Siwa, Liza Koshy . . . There were loads of people there. It was so much fun; I absolutely loved it.

SATURDAY

HARVEY: Our first lie-in! Sooo good.

MAX: We had the morning off so we woke up late, and then met up with Amelia and Houssein and Jackson. We have some Orbeez from yesterday – the ones we stole at the Featured Creator night! We have, like, 2,500 so we wanted to make a video of us filling a bathtub with them . . .

HARVEY: It went horribly wrong, as we didn't have enough to fill it up! But we tried. We wanted to get some more, so we went back to the Orbeez stand in the convention – but we made the mistake of telling them what they were for, and they wouldn't let us have any more because they didn't want to get in trouble with the hotel. It was still a fun video to make anyway. It'll be on our channel soon – definitely by the time this book comes out!

MAX: Then, in the afternoon, we hosted the Musical.ly stage again – our friend Sophie from *America's Got Talent* performed, and it was really fun. After that we performed on the AwesomenessTV stage. At first there weren't many people there – probably about 200 – but by the end of the show we had about 3,000 people watching us! It was amazing. And that was our last event of VidCon! I have honestly had the best time. It's crazy here. It was fun at VidCon Europe and at Playlist – but this is just on a different scale. I'm half looking forward to going home, half really sad to be leaving.

SUNDAY

MAX: Today was our last day and it was insane – we went to a Musical.ly pool party. It was in a secret location because they didn't want anyone crashing.

HARVEY: I think it was in Bel Air – but we had to be driven there by shuttle to keep the location secret. We got there early, before it got really busy. So obviously we started doing flips off a fountain, which is in a lot of our Musical.lys! It was a lot of fun. The party was in this mansion with an amazing pool.

MAX: JiffPom was there – he was so cute! And his owners were really nice too.

HARVEY: He is the coolest dog ever – I know it sounds harsh but he's a lot cooler than our dogs. Cooler than us! He can do handstands and dabs and is just incredible – I can barely walk sometimes! And he's just a tiny dog! It's amazing. I loved meeting him – he's adorable. It's on our Instagram.

MAX: And then we went straight to the airport!

HARVEY: It was the worst flight ever. There was no in-flight entertainment – so we had an eleven-hour flight with nothing to do. We forgot books too! It was sooo boring. And, as always, I couldn't sleep on the plane. *And* I was sitting in the aisle seat so people kept banging into me on their way to the toilet. It was such a terrible flight! But I'm pleased to be going home. We missed our dad and our siblings. I'm kind of used to not seeing Leo all the time, but I was sad to be away from Dad and Tilly.

MAX: I'm looking forward to seeing the dogs again – that's a good thing about going home. Freddie is being so annoying at the moment. But Pippa was a lot worse when she was a puppy, so we're just waiting for Freddie to grow up. We have school tomorrow, which is a very painful thought. I can't wait for the summer holidays. Homework is what gets me. I want to do filming – but then I remember I have to work and it's so annoying. It's funny coming back to reality. It doesn't feel weird to be back at school or at home; it feels normal. But it was fun to be in California for a week. I guess we're just really lucky we can do both.

BBC FILMING

MAX: Things are quite quiet now. We did some filming for our documentary outside school – we couldn't shoot inside because that would invade other kids' privacy. We were being natural – just having a chat with our friends, surrounded by cameras! I'm enjoying doing the show even more than I thought I would. It feels like we're learning something.

HARVEY: It's such a cool opportunity for us. We know we're lucky. Being filmed is more complicated than I thought though! Obviously being able to work with a camera crew around is a good skill to learn, but you also have to remember random stuff – like if you're walking somewhere you have to make sure the camera isn't behind you, or reflecting in your sunglasses or something. And if you get something wrong you have to do it over and over again. Even if we're just talking normally to each other and we mess up a sentence, which we would do in real life, we have to do it again. One thing I've learned is that you can't just assume people understand exactly what you're talking about. You have to be precise about the details – otherwise they'll have no idea what you're on about!

MAX: The crew are all so great, so it's just really fun to hang out with them. We haven't done it that many times – it's definitely not every day or anything like that – but every time we do it we really enjoy it, and we learn something new every time.

HARVEY: Everyone's so nice and it's interesting to learn what different people do too. Obviously there's someone with the camera – we've had Jane, who's the main camera-woman, from the beginning in Amsterdam. And then there's another guy who's the second camera-man – he gets all the angle shots and that kind of stuff. We've had three different sound guys. And we've had two different people called Sarah. The Sarahs are sort of like the managers; that's not their actual title, but they kind of organize everything that's going on – where the team stays and stuff. And they also get people to sign things to say they don't mind being in the TV programme. Every time we talk to someone they have to sign something to say that they're allowed to be on TV.

MAX: See – we're learning a lot!

GO RUN FOR FUN

MAX: Go Run for Fun was such a great event – I loved it. It was so organized. It was set up to encourage primary school kids to get involved in running and being active. It was kind of like a charity event, and it was at the Olympic Park in London, which was really cool.

HARVEY: We stayed in London on Saturday night and then went to the event on Sunday morning. Everyone was so high-energy – the atmosphere was amazing. We did the warm-ups onstage with some actual Olympians – Denise Lewis, Colin Jackson and Amy Tinkler. Denise has won gold in the heptathlon, Colin won silver for athletics, and Amy won bronze for gymnastics. So – slightly better at sport than us! It was lovely to meet them. The warm-up was a lot of fun – we did it to 'Uptown Funk'.

MAX: There were two sessions, with 2,500 kids in each – one in the morning and one in the afternoon. We got to use the air horn for the start of the race! And

then hold the tape at the finish line. We also sang 'Counting Stars', 'Words' and 'Sweet Lovin'' – one of our own songs and two covers for kids who didn't know who we were, so they could still enjoy it. There was such an amazing sound system – Harvey and I actually sounded good!

HARVEY: I was so hungry after the warm-up in the morning that I had to go to Westfield and buy loads of food – then I couldn't eat all of it! Don't shop when you're hungry! It was a really fun event though.

MAX: Some of the kids ran insanely fast – one of them ran a mile in, like, eight minutes! And they're at primary school! I think you can probably guess . . . Harvey and I did *not* run.

MANCHESTER FOR THE WEEKEND: BE SEEN IN GREEN DAY AND CBBC SUMMER SOCIAL

FRIDAY

HARVEY: We've just been doing school stuff recently, which is fine. Term is coming to an end so it's going to be a lot more relaxed. We have a trip with our choir to Croatia next week, then we only have two more days and we're done!

MAX: School is school – it can be fun, but sometimes it can be a bit dull. That's a schoolkid's life: you just have to put up with it!

HARVEY: But after school on Thursday we drove up to Manchester and stayed in a hotel, and then the next day we surprised a primary school for Be Seen in Green Day! The school had won our competition, so we went to sing for them. It was so nice to meet them all. They'd been signed up by one of their

students, a girl who'd been on the children's ward in the Royal Manchester Hospital, so it was really special to meet her.

MAX: We did an assembly and they asked us questions afterwards. We sang 'Be Seen in Green' together and it was awesome – the kids were very loud! After the assembly we went round the classrooms and took pictures with all the different classes. It was really fun.

HARVEY: Then we went to the hospital, where we visited loads of kids and gave a prize to the ward that was greenest!

MAX: We put the whole thing on Musical.ly. We started with a performance of 'Be Seen in Green' in the main hall and then we went round to see everyone individually.

HARVEY: It was really nice to meet all the kids – there was a pug called Alfie going around kids too. We did a challenge: that we would sing any song they requested, whether we knew it or not. One girl asked for 'Troublemaker' by Olly Murs, which is an amazing song, but unfortunately neither of us had played it before, so that was really hard!

MAX: We went to several wards, with about fifteen kids in each. It's great to see how music can lift someone's spirits, even if they're having a terrible day. One boy amazed me – he was about five and we think he should become a comedian. We said, 'Do you like to sing?' and he said, 'No, I'd like to dance!' So we asked him to dance with us. He jumped out of bed and said, 'Mum, where's my shoes?' And we told him we were going to play some music, and he said, 'NO, NO, NO! LET ME GET MY SHOES!' And then he danced and he was so cute. It was really fun. We posted a Musical.ly with another boy we met. And now he's getting massive! We're so proud of him. He asked us how to get followers and stuff, and we told him to just keep uploading and doing different things and he's doing it. It's amazing. All the kids there are incredible. There was this little two-year-old who just loved music and dancing. She didn't know who we were but she loved people coming in to sing to her. The whole day was really fun and inspirational. So much singing, and so much green! Some of the kids even dyed their hair!

HARVEY: We also got to sell ice cream in an ice-cream van outside the hospital – literally every kid's dream! Max was all right at it but I was rubbish!

It's harder than you think! It comes out of the machine so fast – it's really tricky to get right! Because of the theme of the day we put green sauce on it, which was fun – though it didn't look very good on mine!

MAX: Funnily enough, working in an ice-cream van is something I've always wanted to do. The first ice cream I made was terrible – it was all dripping down my hands – but the last ones were great! Harvey was really bad at it. There's evidence on Instagram. It was such a great day.

HARVEY: We then went out for our cousins' birthdays – they're three and six but their birthdays are on the same day, which is weird. Although I guess Max and I have our birthday on the same day . . . but that's less weird because we're twins! And at our uncle's house we did a music video for 'Smells Like Teen Spirit' by Nirvana with him. We've put it on YouTube now too. It was really fun.

SATURDAY

MAX: Today we went to the CBBC Summer Social. I had no idea how much fun it was going to be – I loved it. I didn't know we were going to be involved in so much TV stuff and so much performing.

HARVEY: It was in BBC Media City in Manchester. There were loads of characters from CBBC and lots of fun stuff to do. They were broadcasting it live, and we did a twin Q&A, and then we did a set – so many of our fans were there, plus some very little kids!

MAX: Performing was exciting. A lot of people there were really little or didn't know us – but they really enjoyed our performance, even without having heard of us. We met loads of CBBC hosts, which was awesome. It was especially great to meet Hacker T. Dog – I love him! As soon as it finished we drove home. It was a really fun day!

CROATIA

SUNDAY

HARVEY: We're driving to Croatia for a school trip. I'm not really sure what to expect – last year we went on a trip to Germany, which was fourteen hours on the coach and I hated that journey, so this one will be interesting! It's a music trip, and over five days we're going to do two or three performances. The rest of the time it's basically a holiday. The last one was really fun (apart from the coach) so the drive will hopefully be worth it . . .!

MAX: Also, Germany wasn't sunny. So I'm really looking forward to Croatia. The shows will be amazing. I really hope it's going to be fun. Tilly is on standby to take over on our Musical.ly account – it'll be so cute and funny. She's not cute in real life, in my opinion, but she is so good on video. Last year, when we were away and had no Wi-Fi, Mum suggested she run our account, and Tilly loved it. If we can't get any signal in Croatia, that's the plan again!

MONDAY

MAX: The coach journey was long and boring. We left on Sunday afternoon and got here on Monday afternoon.

HARVEY: It was twenty-eight hours so we slept overnight. Or tried to – I shared a pillow with the friend I was sitting with, but we kept bumping heads. In the end I just let him have it!

MAX: When we got here, we put all the instruments away (there were loads, as it was a music trip) and went to our rooms, which were like mini apartments. It was really nice! Usually we stay in hostels.

HARVEY: Unfortunately the food where we were staying wasn't great. It never is on school trips! But Croatia was beautiful. We were right next to the sea and we got to go down to the beach, which was cool.

TUESDAY

HARVEY: We had breakfast (again, not great), but on the up side there's a massive pool with a slide, and a volleyball court and a trampoline.

MAX: We went swimming for a couple of hours, which was fun. After that we rehearsed for the show. Harvey and I will just be singing 'Pencil Full of Lead' by Paolo Nutini so we aren't on for very long. Then we visited Europe's biggest cave, which is in Slovenia. It was really cool! The train goes down into it for five kilometres! It was so cold. We walked around, and then at the end there's this room where they do concerts because the acoustics are amazing. Our school choir performed there and it sounded so good!

HARVEY: The cave was pretty cool – although after a while the rocks did kind of look the same! We went out for dinner and the food was a lot better.

WEDNESDAY

MAX: This morning we spent another two hours in the pool. Then we rehearsed in a nearby town where we were going to perform. We got to go shopping, and I bought a laser pen! Later we performed to about 500 people. And it was so cool – about fifteen minutes before the concert Harvey posted on Instagram, and then about fifty fans came to see us! We didn't expect to have any fans in Croatia and it was so lovely to see them, and really surprising. The show went really well, and then, after we'd packed up the instruments, lots of people asked for pictures – it was so nice to meet them (and we got out of doing the heavy lifting!).

HARVEY: The show was in the town square. It was amazing that there were fans, but also a really great audience for the whole school. Croatian people are very friendly!

THURSDAY

MAX: Obviously we went swimming in the morning. Then we visited another town and went shopping again.

HARVEY: I bought a watermelon and rolled it down the street. It was huge and weighed a ton, and it only cost £5! I accidentally dropped it off the balcony of our apartment, and that was funny – luckily no one was hurt. It exploded everywhere! I'm definitely going to put that on YouTube! We weren't expecting to have any signal, but it was really good, so we could post all week – we didn't need Tilly to do it for us. Luckily!

MAX: That night we performed in the restaurant at our apartment, and everyone sounded good. We didn't announce this performance – our teachers wouldn't have been very happy if fans had turned up! We got spotted once or twice though, and that was unexpected. It's so nice meeting people who know us.

FRIDAY

MAX: A twenty-eight-hour coach journey back home again! The trip out was not fun – you're looking forward to getting there so the time goes really slowly, and I was cranky and tired. On the way back it felt a lot quicker and I was in a much better mood!

HARVEY: The coach journey wasn't great – but we did get burgers! I've been thinking about food a lot on this trip!

LAST DAYS OF SCHOOL

MAX: We got back on Saturday and had a day off on Sunday – then school on Monday! It was pretty chilled – it was end-of-term vibes. There wasn't too much actual studying.

HARVEY: It wasn't fun going back in on Monday! I was so tired and we'd only had one day to recover. Luckily I got to work in reception carrying lost property around – I was first to volunteer! So I got to miss a few lessons.

MAX: Tuesday was a half-day: we came home and relaxed.

HARVEY: SO glad it's the summer holidays now! We're going to America again soon – I can't wait.

MAX: And we're going to perform at Camp Bestival tomorrow, which should be fun – although the weather forecast isn't great . . . !

THINGS MAX AND HARVEY LOVE ABOUT THEIR SUMMER HOLIDAYS

MAX:

1. Being in LA
2. Going to Disney
3. Performing at Camp Bestival
4. Going to Playlist DC

HARVEY:

1. Warmth
2. Relaxing
3. Fun
4. Spending time with friends
5. NO SCHOOL

CAMP BESTIVAL

MAX: The weather is not on our side! We've been going to Camp Bestival, which is like a music festival for families, for the last five years. It's really fun: we camp with our family and some friends and see lots of acts. This year we're performing too! Before, we've always had to lug our stuff from the car park to the campsite, which usually takes up the whole of the first day. This year we stayed in the artists' campsite. Last year we had just hit a million fans on Musical.ly: people kept finding our tent and recognizing us. Now that our following has quadrupled, we wanted to be more private. It was only a ten-minute walk to our campsite, so that was a lot easier! It was so muddy though!

HARVEY: We performed on the Friday. We were worried we'd have a really low turnout. I'm not complaining or anything – we were really grateful – but we were on at midday, when people are usually having lunch. We were in the biggest tent as well, and it would've looked really empty if no one had come. But we were amazed – we had, like, 3,000 people there. Lots of them didn't know who we were, but the ones at the front definitely did – they

were really responsive and lovely. We did about seven songs – I hope people liked them! It was amazing.

MAX: It was so windy and rainy – tents were blowing all over the place. The one we were playing in was the only proper shelter. The rain started up again when we were on and everyone came in to take cover, so we ended up with about 3,000 people watching us by mistake! It was so, so fun. I loved it. Over the weekend Louisa Johnson, Ann Marie and Mark Ronson were playing in the same place and we were really pleased we basically got the same crowd as those guys! But that night was horrible, weather-wise. Our campsite wasn't that bad (except around the toilets), but in the arena there was no grass left – only mud. No matter where you walked, your shoes got muddy. I ruined two pairs of shoes. We watched Mark Ronson – he was amazing.

HARVEY: Mark was so nice – he was talking to everyone. And his show was great. I didn't know what to expect, but it was like a really cool DJ set.

We got a photo with him for Instagram and he was so nice about it. I really liked him.

MAX: We also got to meet Ann Marie, who was really nice too: she took a photo of us, then went over to meet her fans and didn't leave until everyone was happy. And then she did a Musical.ly with us, which was so cool! And we spoke to Louisa – though we couldn't get a photo. She's really friendly and such an amazing singer. We met Madness too!

HARVEY: Our dad was really jealous.

MAX: By Saturday, everything was mud, no matter where you walked. It was still a fun day, and we did a meet-and-greet, which had a really good turnout – I think about three or four hundred people!

HARVEY: There was a miscommunication somewhere – we were supposed to have a fairly big tent for our meet-and-greet, but there was a band rehearsing in it! So we were told to use a smaller one – and then 300 people turned up and it was so cramped! It was hilarious – and so, so nice to meet everyone.

MAX: It was great to meet so many of our fans at a festival.

HARVEY: That night we went to a silent disco: there's no overall sound system; instead everyone has a set of headphones and there are competing DJs. You choose whose set to listen to. We found that Dick and Dom were doing one set! They were playing amazing songs – like Kaiser Chiefs and stuff, so we all chose them. I felt bad for the other guy, but they were great. And who wouldn't choose Dick and Dom?

MAX: I love Camp Bestival, it's amazing: such a great atmosphere, and the food's good too. Even though the weather was just horrendous, it was so much fun.

HARVEY: At the end there was a firework display, which was really impressive. They do it every year, and this was the best. It's in the grounds of this massive castle, and they projected a really cool animation on to it. It was awesome.

MAX AND HARVEY'S HIGHLIGHTS OF THE YEAR

1. VidCon Anaheim
2. Camp Bestival
3. Playlist Orlando
4. Shorty Awards
5. Playlist DC

WHAT'S NEXT?

MAX:

1. Release more songs
2. Meeting more and more fans
3. Doing more and more performances

HARVEY:

1. Hopefully we'll have an EP by the end of the year
2. The release of our documentary (and book!)

THE END –

AND THANK YOU

MAX: And now we're off to America and this book has to go off to print, so this is the end!

HARVEY: We're doing lots of shows across the US so we'll be away for ages. I really wish we could share it with you, but this book has to go to the printer.

MAX: I'm really sad about that – it's been so much fun making a record of everything we've been up to. I think we'll always look back on this year, and I love sharing it with you guys. We never would have been able to do it without you, so thank you so much.

HARVEY: This has been such a cool year for us. We've never done this much, ever. A couple of years ago I would never have imagined it could happen – let alone doing a book where we talk about it all. I really hope that we can carry on with everything and keep meeting our fans, who make it all possible. But even if we can't, then this book will always be a reminder of what we did. Thank you so, so much for supporting us.

PUFFIN BOOKS

UK | USA | Canada | Ireland | Australia
India | New Zealand | South Africa

Puffin Books is part of the Penguin Random House group of companies
whose addresses can be found at global.penguinrandomhouse.com.

www.penguin.co.uk
www.puffin.co.uk
www.ladybird.co.uk

First published 2017

003

Text copyright © Max and Harvey Mills, 2017

Illustrations by Jan Bielecki

The moral right of the author and illustrator has been asserted

Typeset in ITC Avant Garde by Janene Spencer

Printed in Great Britain by Clays Ltd, St Ives plc

A CIP catalogue record for this book is available from the British Library

ISBN: 978–0–141–38799–4

All correspondence to:
Puffin Books
Penguin Random House Children's
80 Strand, London WC2R 0RL

THE END –

AND THANK YOU

MAX: And now we're off to America and this book has to go off to print, so this is the end!

HARVEY: We're doing lots of shows across the US so we'll be away for ages. I really wish we could share it with you, but this book has to go to the printer.

MAX: I'm really sad about that – it's been so much fun making a record of everything we've been up to. I think we'll always look back on this year, and I love sharing it with you guys. We never would have been able to do it without you, so thank you so much.

HARVEY: This has been such a cool year for us. We've never done this much, ever. A couple of years ago I would never have imagined it could happen – let alone doing a book where we talk about it all. I really hope that we can carry on with everything and keep meeting our fans, who make it all possible. But even if we can't, then this book will always be a reminder of what we did. Thank you so, so much for supporting us.

PUFFIN BOOKS

UK | USA | Canada | Ireland | Australia
India | New Zealand | South Africa

Puffin Books is part of the Penguin Random House group of companies
whose addresses can be found at global.penguinrandomhouse.com.

www.penguin.co.uk
www.puffin.co.uk
www.ladybird.co.uk

First published 2017

003

Text copyright © Max and Harvey Mills, 2017

Illustrations by Jan Bielecki

The moral right of the author and illustrator has been asserted

Typeset in ITC Avant Garde by Janene Spencer

Printed in Great Britain by Clays Ltd, St Ives plc

A CIP catalogue record for this book is available from the British Library

ISBN: 978-0-141-38799-4

All correspondence to:
Puffin Books
Penguin Random House Children's
80 Strand, London WC2R 0RL